# Native American Shipwrecks

**James P. Delgado**

*Watts* LIBRARY

**Franklin Watts**
A Division of Grolier Publishing
New York • London • Hong Kong • Sydney
Danbury, Connecticut

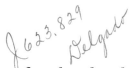
*To children's librarians everywhere for what they do to inspire us all to learn at an early age. This book is particularly for Nancy Goodhart, children's librarian and mother. Thanks also to Vickie Jensen, Rachel Grant, Chris Amer, and Jonathan Leader.*

**Note to readers:** Definitions for words in **bold** can be found in the Glossary at the back of this book.

Photographs ©: Alton Lowe: 26; AP/Wide World Photos: 50, 51 (Elaine Thompson); Bancroft Library, University of California, Berkeley: 40; California State University, Los Angeles: 13 (Naval Air Weapons Station, Point Mugu, CA/Pat Martz); Corbis-Bettmann: 3 bottom (Nathan Benn), 49 (Richard A. Cooke), 41 (Werner Forman), 10, 20 (Wolfgang Kaehler), 36 (Layne Kennedy), 38 (Charles & Josette Lenars), 11, 24 (Galen Rowell), 42, 43 (Gian Berto Vanni), 32, 33; Courtesy of J. Leader, South Carolina Institute of Archeology and Anthropology: 30, 31 (Columbia Photo); Courtesy of James P. Delgado: 6, 7 (Gary Davis); East Carolina University, Greenville, NC: 3 top, 14, 17, 19 bottom (David S. Phelps, PhD, Coastal Archaeology Office); Liaison Agency, Inc.: 25 (Alissa Crandall), 23 (Hulton Getty); Makah Cultural and Research Center: 53 (Yasu Osawa), 44, 46, 47 (Washington State University); National Geographic Image Collection: 4, 5 (Thad Samuels Abell II), 28 (James Stanfield); New York Public Library Picture Collection: 34 (Harper's Young People, July 29, 1890); North Wind Picture Archives: 8; Pettigrew State Park: 19 top.

Cover illustration by Greg Harris.

Visit Franklin Watts on the Internet at: http://publishing.grolier.com

**Library of Congress Cataloging-in-Publication Data**

Delgado, James P.
    Native American shipwrecks / James P. Delgado.
        p.        cm.— (Watts Library)
    Includes bibliographical references and index.
    Summary: Examines archaeological excavations of the watercraft of ancient Native Americans and what the findings tell us about the daily life and culture of people who lived thousands of years ago.
    ISBN: 0-531-20379-4 (lib. bdg.)        0-531-16473-x (pbk.)
    1. Indians—Boats Juvenile literature. 2. Indians—Antiquities Juvenile literature. 3. Canoes and canoeing Juvenile literature. 4. Skin boats Juvenile literature. 5. Kayaks Juvenile literature. 6. Excavations (Archaeology) Juvenile literature. [1. Indians—Boats. 2. Indians—Antiquities. 3. Indian craft. 4. Canoes and canoeing. 5. Excavations (Archaeology) 6. Underwater archaeology. 7. Archaeology.] I. Title. II. Series.
E59.C2D45  2000
623.8'29'08997—dc21                                          99-25886
                                                            CIP

# Contents

*A researcher investigates the remains of a burial site.*

# Into the Deep

I grew up in San Jose, a fast-growing city near San Francisco Bay. When I was ten, my family moved to a new house in an area that had been farms and orchards for more than 100 years. When we moved in, for miles in every direction, bulldozers were digging streets and foundations for all the new houses.

The bulldozers stopped one day. They had uncovered an ancient Indian village. Stone bowls, arrowheads, bone tools, and human skeletons from burial sites lay everywhere. **Archaeologists** came to record the findings and conduct an emergency dig. I had been reading about ancient Egypt in school. Archaeology fascinated me. So I asked the archaeologists if I could help them. They said yes!

From that time on, I have been hooked. I started by working in the hot sun, sorting and washing stone tools. Soon they let me work in the trenches with them, digging up ancient burial sites and houses. Sitting on the dirt with a small trowel in my hand, I removed layers of dirt to look into the empty eye sockets of someone who had died 3,000 years ago. I studied ancient history and archaeology every chance I had. I went to college and found another great interest—the ocean.

I learned how to scuba dive and discovered that the sea is filled with traces of the past. Now I work underwater as an archaeologist, finding wrecked ships and flooded sites where ancient people lived thousands of years ago.

—James P. Delgado

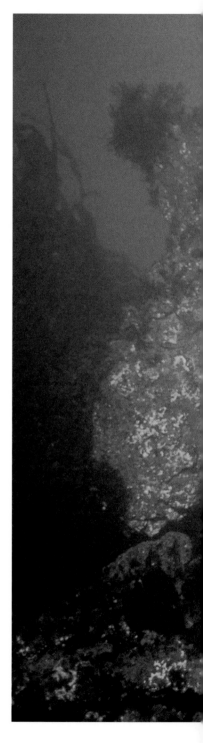

*Underwater archaeologist
James P. Delgado at work*

*Many early Native Americans lived and hunted near lakes, rivers, and the sea.*

# Chapter One

# Boats of the Native Americans

People have lived in the Americas for tens of thousands of years. They may have come here from Asia. They may also have originated here. Their stories refer to Raven, Coyote, and other creators. No matter how they arrived, they have been here a long time.

Native Americans tell stories of their ancestors' lives and beliefs. These stories

## What Were Native American Boats Made Of?

Boats, rafts, and canoes were important to many of the early Native American groups. They built these craft with whatever they had at hand and from nature. Some Indians hollowed and carved logs to make canoes. Others split logs into planks and tied them together. Still others stripped bark off trees to make canoes. Some made boats out of animal hides, while others used grass and reeds that grow in salt marshes and lakes (above).

keep the memories of the past alive. Archaeologists also study the past.

Archaeologists have been studying Native American people for more than 100 years. They dig into the ground to discover ancient campfires and settlements. They study large stone and clay cities built into cliffs in the American Southwest. They map large earth mounds. They clear the jungle away from stone cities and pyramids. They study stone and bone tools and pottery. And from time to time, they discover ancient canoes and parts of boats.

## Boat Uses

With their boats, canoes, and kayaks, early Native Americans traveled long distances by water. The Inuit of the Arctic spread throughout the North, using kayaks and large skin boats called **umiaks** in the summer when the ice retreated. Other peoples made long journeys on other coasts. The Haida of British Columbia, Canada, built large oceangoing canoes. In these canoes, they paddled hundreds, even thousands, of

*Present-day Inuit whalers paddle an umiak, a sealskin boat, in the Arctic Ocean near Barrow, Alaska.*

miles. The Ohlone from San Francisco Bay built large boats from reeds known as **tules**. In their tule boats, they sailed out past the Golden Gate to hunt and fish on the Farallone Islands, 26 miles (42 kilometers) off the coast.

Other Native Americans used their boats to harvest the sea. From their canoes, the Haida used long wooden rakes in water more than 30 feet (9 meters) deep to gather long, horn-shaped shells called **dentalia**. They then traded these shells to other Indians as far away as the Great Plains, which is thousands of miles away. Many used their boats to fish. The Wampanoag of Nantucket, Massachusetts, like the Makah on the Straits of Juan de Fuca in Washington state, hunted whales in their canoes. The Inuit hunted walruses, seals, and whales such as the **beluga** from their kayaks.

## Proving the Existence of Native American Boats

Archaeologists have discovered that the ancient peoples of the Americas used boats even when no trace of boats has survived. How do they know? Archaeologists found carved stone models and toys. They have **excavated** fishing and whaling equipment made of stone, bone, and shell. And they have found ancient settlements on offshore islands that could have been reached only by boats.

In southern California, for example, archaeologists have discovered that the first peoples reached San Nicolas Island, 75 miles (121 km) off the coast, some 6,000 years ago. Their

boats are long gone, but their settlements on the island are proof that they had oceangoing craft.

Some of the first Native American peoples are now gone, victims of disease and war. Some were forced away from the lands they lived on for thousands of years. But many others have survived. Native Americans have made kayaks, canoes, and other boats throughout the centuries. Many Native Americans still make these boats today. They are preserving an ancient tradition.

*Archaeologists in California unearthed evidence of Indian settlements on San Nicolas Island, proving that early Native Americans traveled on the ocean.*

13

*A wooden canoe excavated from the bottom of Lake Phelps*

# Chapter Two

# Log Boats in the Lake

In 1985, visitors to Pettigrew State Park in North Carolina told park rangers that they had found stone tools, pieces of clay pots, and wooden canoes. Their discoveries were all at one end of Lake Phelps. The water in the lake was low because of a **drought**. The water was the lowest it had been for a long time, perhaps even hundreds of years. Rangers called in archaeologists to take a look.

The archaeologists discovered twenty-six dugout canoes. It is the largest group

15

*Archaeology students remove sediment from one of the sunken Lake Phelps canoes with a suction hose. White stakes mark the position of the canoe.*

of Native American craft known to have survived. A major archaeological find, the canoes of Lake Phelps date back thousands of years.

## Lake Phelps Canoes

The canoes were made from large cypress logs that were burned to make a soft spot in the middle and then scraped to hollow them out. In the laboratory, archaeologists can tell the age of ancient organic material by a special method called **radiocarbon dating**. Because all of the Lake Phelps canoes had been partly burned, archaeologists were able to find out how old all of them were. The oldest canoe was more than 4,000 years old.

The canoe came from a time the archaeologists call the Late Archaic period, which began 5,000 years ago and lasted

2,000 years. Because the climate had warmed up after the last Ice Age, there was more food to be found, population had grown, and people began visiting Lake Phelps more frequently.

Other Lake Phelps canoes came from the Early Woodland period, which started 3,000 years ago and lasted 1,000 years. The Early Woodland people made pottery. One broken pot was found partly inside and partly outside one of the canoes. Radiocarbon dating showed archaeologists that the canoe came from the Early Woodland period, and that the pot, from a later period, had fallen and broken on the edge of the abandoned canoe.

Many of the canoes—eleven of them—date back to the Middle Woodland period, which began 2,300 years ago and lasted 1,100 years. Large family groups settled on the northern and western shores of the lake in the summer and fall. They hunted, fished, and gathered wild plants. With so many canoes surviving from this period, the archaeologists were able to see a pattern. That is,

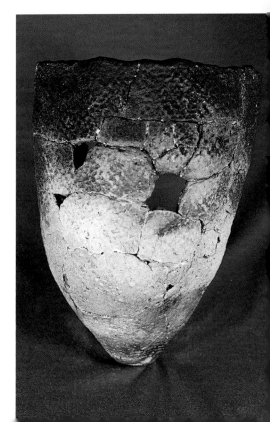

*This reconstructed cooking pot from the Middle Woodland period was found broken partly inside and partly outside one of the canoes in Lake Phelps.*

they were able to see how often canoes were built and how long they lasted. Of these eleven canoes, eight were made between A.D. 110 and 340. Radiocarbon dating showed they had been built twenty to thirty years apart.

By the Late Woodland period, which ended 300 years ago, not many people were living on or using the lake. Only three canoes dated from this period. The youngest canoe of these three was nearly 600 years old, and the oldest was 800 years old.

# Artifacts

Near the canoes and on the shore, archaeologists found many **artifacts**, including stone tools and clay pots. Most of the artifacts, like the canoes, came from the Middle Woodland period. Very few date to the Late Woodland period.

The stone and clay artifacts suggest that people were not using the lake as much as their ancestors had, mostly because they depended more on farming at their permanent towns. When the first European settlers found Lake Phelps in 1755, there were no Native Americans there. They had completely abandoned the lake as their population declined. But in the water, out of sight and undiscovered until more than 200 years later, was archaeological evidence that people had lived, fished, and hunted on the lake for thousands of years before the first Europeans arrived.

*Pottery pieces from the Lake Phelps site*

*These spear and arrow points prove that Native Americans hunted on Lake Phelps thousands of years before the first white settlers.*

*An Inuit man steers a wooden kayak.*

# Chapter Three

# Skin Boats of the Frozen North

When early European explorers reached the Arctic at the top of the world, they encountered Native Americans in boats made out of animal skin. These skin boats were one of the earliest kinds of Native American boats. They are called kayaks.

Archaeologists working in the Arctic have found evidence of early kayaks as far back as A.D. 500. Some archaeologists suspect that the kayak may actually date back another 2,500 years. That would make the kayak one of the world's oldest and longest surviving types of boat.

# The Invention of Kayaks

The kayak appears to be an invention of the original inhabitants of the shores of the Bering Sea. As they migrated east into Arctic Canada, they brought kayaks with them. They also used the larger umiaks. Archaeologists digging on a beach in Arctic Greenland discovered a 500-year-old umiak. Archaeologists believe that there may still be other ancient craft buried on other Arctic beaches.

Underwater archaeologists have never found a kayak wreck. Because of the light, fragile nature of early kayaks, only a few fragments of them have survived. To find evidence of ancient kayaks, archaeologists look at ancient campsites for sea mammal bones and harpoon parts, which show that the people were using kayaks to hunt on the water. They also look for small wood and ivory models of kayaks. These models appear to have been good-luck charms to ensure safe use of kayaks, which capsized easily.

# Kayak Design

Beginning with Martin Frobisher in 1576, early European explorers in the Arctic frequently remarked on kayaks and the larger umiaks. As European explorers pushed deeper into the Arctic, they encountered different styles. All kayaks conformed to a basic design, however. This design does not seem to have changed for more than 2,000 years. Traditional kayak builders can still make a kayak in the ancient way.

An Inuit hunter built a kayak with a driftwood-and-bone frame that he pegged with pins made of wood or bone and tied together with animal skin. The major parts are a backbone called a **keelson**, the frame or ribs, and the cross beams. Most kayaks were covered with caribou skin or sealskin. It took the

*An Alaskan umiak made of sealskin stretched over a wooden frame dries in the sun.*

## Inuit Kayak Terms

**Aja at**—the cross beams of a boat
**Kujak**—the long structure fastened to the bottom of a boat to brace the frame
**Tikpik**—the frame or ribs of a boat

skin of five caribou or nine seals to cover the average kayak. The skin was usually replaced every year. Seal oil was used to waterproof the skin.

Usually only men used kayaks, although Inuit traditions note that women were occasionally taught to use a kayak. It was an exception and considered a great honor or act of love by a father or husband. We know from early explorers that Inuit men were considered active and productive hunters only if they hunted with a kayak. From kayaks, they hunted sea mammals, waterfowl, and moose or caribou swimming in the shallows.

Kayaks were important. An Inuit man's major possessions were his kayak, a tent, a sled, and his dogs. Early explorers

## Today's Kayaks

Kayaks continue to have great appeal today. Very few of today's kayaks are made in the traditional way with wood, bone, and skin. But people throughout the Americas build and use modern kayaks made of plastic, canvas, wood, metal, or fiberglass.

were able to trade for kayaks, which they took home with them.

There are kayaks more than 200 years old in European museums. Canadian and U.S. museums also have kayaks. Most of these are only about 100 years old. Thanks to archaeology, we know that the kayak dates back thousands of years.

*Lucayan traders traveling by canoe in the Caribbean*

# Chapter Four

# The Canoe from the Blue Hole

When Christopher Columbus arrived in the Americas in 1492, he called the people he met "Indians." In fact, they were a Caribbean people now called Lucayan. Sadly, there are no Lucayan left alive. For twenty years after Columbus arrived, Spanish settlers conquered and enslaved the Lucayan. Tens of thousands of Lucayan were killed by soldiers or disease,

## The Lucayan

Archaeologists have been studying the Lucayan for years. They have learned about these vanished people by digging up the abandoned sites of Lucayan villages. The ancestors of the Lucayan lived on the banks of the Orinoco River in Venezuela in South America. About 2,000 years ago, the ancestors of the Lucayan took to the sea and spread to the islands of the Caribbean. Archaeologists know this because the Lucayan made a type of pottery that no other Native American group did. They have found this pottery at the oldest village sites in Venezuela. They have traced it through newer village sites in Puerto Rico, Cuba, Jamaica, Haiti, the Dominican Republic, Turks and Caicos, and the Bahamas, where they unearthed these fragments of Indian pottery.

or they died working as slaves in Spanish mines. By 1520, there were no more Lucayan.

Because there are no more Lucayan, archaeologists have studied books and letters written by the Spaniards who first met them and then conquered and killed them. Archaeologists compare Spanish accounts with what they find in their excavations. The Lucayan lived in large houses with many families under the same roof. The villages were close to the sea. The Lucayan farmed, hunted, and fished. They had a complex political system, traded with other people far away, and fought fierce wars.

The Spanish explorers wrote about large Lucayan canoes. Columbus wrote about seeing a Lucayan canoe as large as one of his small ships. He described another canoe that could hold as many as 150 people. The Spaniards also described beautiful, fast canoes that were made for war, for fishing, and for trade with other islands. The Lucayan were skilled navigators and boatbuilders. After they were killed, none of their canoes survived.

## Inside a Blue Hole

In 1995, underwater explorers found a Lucayan canoe sunk 60 feet (18 m) deep inside an underwater cave known as a "blue hole." The cave is on South Andros Island in the Bahamas. The canoe was made from a hollowed log. The explorers also found skeletal remains from as many as sixteen people.

Archaeologists have discovered other Lucayan artifacts in blue holes. This suggests that blue holes were used as Lucayan burial grounds. The Lucayan may have believed the blue holes—deep, dark openings in the bottom of the sea—were gateways to the land of the dead. The canoe may have been a

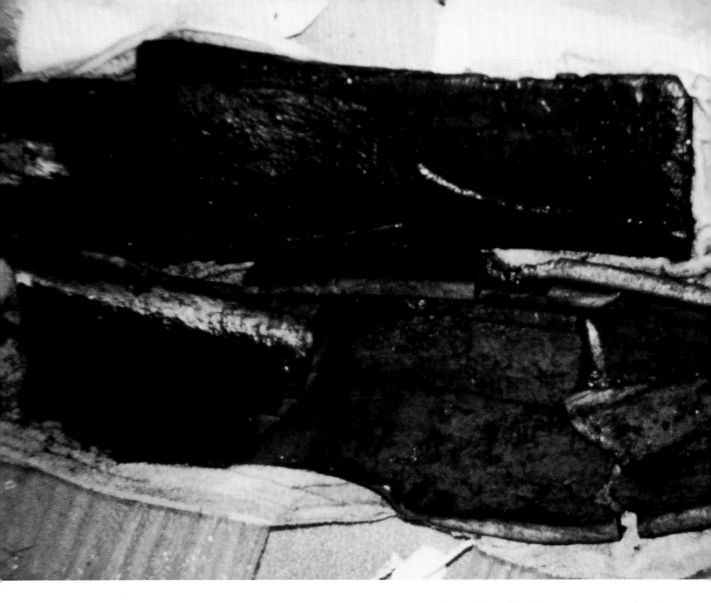

grave offering or may have sunk with a body in it on a final voyage to the underworld.

Archaeologists from the South Carolina Institute of Archaeology and Anthropology were brought in to raise and help preserve the canoe. Only about 6 feet (2 m) of it is left. It is at least 500 years old, dating back to when the last Lucayan were alive. The Lucayan reached the Bahamas about A.D. 900,

*A Lucayan canoe rests on the lifting cradle used to move it from an underwater cave in the Bahamas.*

so the canoe could have been made 1,000 years ago. We will not know for sure until archaeologists finish studying the canoe.

We do know that the canoe from the blue hole is an important underwater archaeological discovery. It has added much more to our knowledge of the canoes and the seafaring of the Lucayan, the first people to meet Columbus.

Native Americans built canoes from the bark of trees.

# Chapter Five

# Bark Canoes

Many Native Americans did not carve canoes out of logs. They used other parts of trees. Indians of eastern North America built canoes out of bark that they stripped off trees. Then they sewed the bark onto a wooden frame. These bark canoes were not heavy. This made them easy for one person to paddle. It also made them easy to carry when the river was too fast or too many rocks were in the way.

Like kayaks and other skin boats, bark canoes did not survive well. There are few traces of these light and fragile craft for archaeologists to find.

## Edwin Tappey Adney

One early student of bark canoes was Edwin Tappey Adney, a nineteen-year-old from Ohio who lived 100 years ago. Adney worked closely with Peter Joe, an Indian from Woodstock, New Brunswick, in Canada, to learn how bark canoes were made.

In 1889, the two men made a birch-bark canoe. Adney made drawings and took notes and published them in an article in *Harper's Young People* magazine. This illustration of Peter Joe is an example of Adney's work.

Edwin Tappey Adney's article is the earliest detailed study of bark canoes. Archaeologists studying bark canoes refer to Adney's article and use his notes, drawings, photographs, and models of canoes.

# How Old Are Bark Canoes?

It is difficult to say how old bark canoes are. They probably date back thousands of years. French explorer Jacques Cartier saw bark canoes almost 500 years ago, in 1535. In 1603, another Frenchman, Samuel de Champlain, exploring near today's Quebec, described bark canoes several yards long that passed his boat easily and quickly. He was impressed. Other Europeans were also impressed and modeled their boats after the Indian design.

Underwater archaeologists have found broken pieces of bark canoes. These canoes capsized and broke up in river **rapids**, where the water surges past sunken rocks or drops over falls. Divers have found many traces of these accidents from long ago. These bark canoes date to a time after European explorers and settlers reached the Americas.

# Fur Traders

European fur traders used Native American canoes and guides to help them on the American frontier. The furs of many animals were important items of trade back then. The **pelts** of the beavers that lived on the banks of the rivers and streams were particularly valuable. The fur trade, which began in the 1600s and continued into the 1800s, was one of the longest lasting and most important commercial activities in the Americas.

*This birch-bark canoe is on display at Minnesota's Grand Portage National Monument, which once served as a fur-trading post.*

Most of the fur trade took place on the Great Lakes, St. Lawrence River, Ottawa River, and hundreds of smaller streams and lakes in the Quetico-Superior area, which is today's Minnesota and Ontario. Centering their activities in North America on the western frontier, the early fur traders used the water as their highway system.

The fragile birch-bark canoes of the fur traders are long gone, smashed and carried away by the strong currents. But archaeologists, with the help of local divers, have found and recovered many artifacts lying on the riverbed. The canoe fragments tell us that the canoes were probably made by Native Americans. They also tell us that the way bark canoes were made then is much the way they are made today by Native Americans. Unlike many other things in the world, bark canoes have not changed much during the thousands of years they have existed.

## What Is Continuity?

When archaeologists find proof that people do not change the way they do things over a long period of time, they call this "continuity." With bark canoes, this means that while various people and cultures came to the Americas through the years, the canoe remains unchanged or little changed.

*A present-day Peruvian fisher in a small reed boat at sunset*

# Chapter Six

# Reed Boats

Native American craft were made with wood, bark, and animal skins. They were also made from plants called reeds. Reeds grow in rivers and lakes and near the ocean in salt marshes. Ancient Egyptians made boats from reeds. Some of these boats were so large and solid that it is believed that they sailed on the open ocean.

Reed boats were made in North America, particularly near San Francisco Bay. The large, shallow bay was surrounded by salt marshes thick with reeds. Reed boats were easy to make, and there were always plenty of reeds. We know about the reed boats in San Francisco

## What Are Reeds?

Reeds are long, hollow grasses that grow in wet areas. They are filled with air, which makes them float.

Bay because Spanish explorers and other Europeans left written descriptions and drawings. The drawings show small rafts that carried two or more people using paddles with blades at each end.

Archaeologists excavating sites on the shores of San Francisco Bay have found that boats played an important role in the lives of the Ohlone people who lived there. The remains of the bones of otters, seals, and fish show that the Ohlone hunted and fished on the water. Stone anchors and fish hooks excavated from bay shore villages are the only archaeological evidence of the reed boats of the Native Americans of San Francisco. They show that boats on the bay could date back as much as 1,500 years.

*The Ohlone hunted and fished in reed boats.*

# Reed Boats in South America

Archaeologists excavating in South America have learned that reed boats farther south date back at least 2,000 years. They have not found remains of the boats, because reeds are so fragile. The boats did not last long before they became soaked with water and broke apart.

Archaeologists have found pottery decorated with drawings of reed boats dating as far back as 2,000 years. The pottery found on the coast of Peru in South America shows boats with a high **prow**, or front end. The design is the same one still used by the Indians of Huanchaco, Pimentel, and Santa Rosa, Peru, on the Pacific coast of South America.

These people continue to make reed boats like those of their ancestors. Like the ancient people, they also use the boats to fish on the ocean. They ride them like a horse, going up and down over the waves. They make new boats

*This spouted ceramic jar showing a fisher in a reed boat dates back almost 2,000 years.*

every year. After the reeds grow tall, boatbuilders cut the green, easy-to-bend reeds and dry them in the sun until they turn a golden brown. The reeds are stiff, but they can still bend. The boatbuilders tie the reeds together in bundles to form a boat with a pointed end that sticks up. This prow helps the boat ride over the waves.

By studying the images on the pottery and working with the people who still build these boats, archaeologists have learned much about ancient reed boats. Like bark canoes and kayaks, the reed boats have lasted, without many changes, for thousands of years.

*A Peruvian boatbuilder ties the dried reeds together in bundles to form a high front end, or prow.*

*Some of the Indian village of Ozette was discovered on the northern coast of Washington.*

# Chapter Seven

# Ozette

In 1970, archaeologists began digging into a hillside on a beach on the northern coast of Washington at a site called Ozette. People had lived there for more than 4,000 years. A portion of the village of Ozette was buried in a landslide of wet clay and water about 500 years ago. At least four large houses and the area around them were covered in an airtight embrace of mud and water.

When archaeologists excavated Ozette, they found more than 50,000 artifacts. Because the artifacts were sealed in mud, archaeologists found many fragile items they had never seen before, such as baskets, clothing, hats, ropes, and sleeping mats. They also found many wood, stone, and shell artifacts.

# Boating People

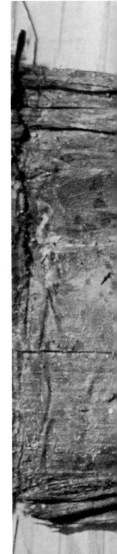

Many artifacts showed that the people of Ozette had lived off the sea, fishing and hunting seals and whales on the open ocean. The archaeologists discovered more than 3,400 whale bones at Ozette. They also found bones from sea otters, seals, porpoises, and deepwater ocean fish such as halibut and herring. The only way the people of Ozette could have caught these fish and that many whales was to go out on the ocean in boats.

Then, as the archaeologists sorted through the thousands of artifacts, they found hundreds of things used in whaling. They discovered harpoons used to spear and kill whales. They found pieces of knives used to take whale blubber off the dead whale. They also found paddles and parts of large wooden canoes that Ozette whalers had taken out to sea.

## Life in Ozette

Because everything inside the flattened houses of Ozette was preserved, archaeologists were able to find out how people had worked in the village. Some weaved clothing and baskets. Others carved wood. Others fished and hunted seals and whales. Some of the artifacts from Ozette were similar to objects found at older archaeological sites, showing that the people of the area had fished and hunted seals and whales for several thousand years.

*A whale harpoon head made out of a mussel shell from the Ozette site*

# The Makah

The people of the Washington coast continued to hunt seals, whales, and fish for hundreds of years after Ozette was partially buried in mud. They continue to live in their ancestral lands today and are now known as the Makah. Explorers and settlers left written accounts, drawings, and later even photographs of Makah whalers and their canoes. The Makah hunted whales until the twentieth century. During the late 1990s, the Makah revived their whaling tradition, but the decision was controversial due to concern for endangered whales.

The canoes of Ozette, like the later canoes of the Makah, were made of large logs. The logs were carved and chopped into shape. The sides were carved thin and steamed with water and fire to extend the wood. The sides were then stretched to make a wide, open canoe.

The Makah boatbuilders made canoes of different sizes and types. They made boats for sealing, whaling, fishing, and trade. In their great canoes, the Makah and other coastal people traveled for hundreds, maybe thousands, of miles on the open ocean. They were great canoe builders and navigators.

Today, we know about Makah and other northwest coast canoes because of archaeological work at sites such as Ozette and early accounts and photographs. Many old canoes were collected for museums in the United States, Canada, and Europe over the last 150 years.

Most of the coastal people, including the Makah, never left. They have kept their traditions and culture alive, and many of them are again building canoes.

*These Makah ivory combs were among the Ozette artifacts.*

*In this 1998 photograph, Makah Indians head into open Pacific Ocean waters in their 32-foot (10-m) canoe, the Hummingbird.*

# Chapter Eight

# Keeping Traditions Alive

People often think of archaeology as the study of people who are dead and forgotten. But archaeologists also study living people. Archaeologists excavate in the heart of modern cities, such as New York, San Francisco, and Montreal. They study how these cities grew and how "modern" Americans live in them.

Archaeologists also study Native Americans. Some of them, such as the Lucayan, are gone. But many other Native American groups continue to thrive, with their traditions and cultures intact and distinct despite 500 years of contact with Europe, Africa, and Asia.

As we have seen, the early boats of the Americas are some of the world's oldest and longest lasting. Kayaks, canoes, and reed boats are still used in the Americas and around the world. Although they are made of modern materials, today's kayaks and canoes are shaped like ancient boats made of skin, bark, and wood. And Native Americans on the coast of Peru continue to make reed boats the same way and with the same materials as their ancestors.

## Boats on Display

Many museums have canoes, kayaks, and other Native American boats in their collections. The Museum of Mankind (London, England), the National Maritime Museum (Greenwich, England), the Canadian Museum of Civilization (Hull, Quebec), the Museum of Anthropology (Vancouver, British Columbia), the National Museum of the American Indian (New York), and hundreds of smaller museums have gathered and preserved Native American craft. It has given people around the world a chance to see and appreciate these canoes, kayaks, and boats and the people who built and used them.

# Living History

Boats inside a glass case in a building have limited benefit though. For many people in the past as well as today, boats were a vibrant part of their culture. Boats helped define who they were as a group. By looking at the artifacts from Ozette and talking to today's Makah people, we know that whaling

*The Makah hunted whales and seals in these canoes at the Makah Museum in Neah Bay, Washington.*

was not just a way to get food. It was part of their religious and political life.

We will never know all there is to know about the Native American boats unless the people who make them share their knowledge. Archaeology can tell only part of the story. Wise archaeologists understand that they study artifacts to learn about people. Part of learning about people means learning *from* them.

# Rebuilding the Past

On the northwest coast of North America, in British Columbia and the states of Washington and Alaska, the local Native Americans have revived their ancient tradition of canoe building and voyaging. For them, it is a way of connecting with the spiritual and cultural life of their ancestors. It is also a way to modernize ancient traditions and link the old canoes and how they were used with life today. The great canoes, once thought extinct, never died.

In some Native American families, knowledge, skill, and traditions were saved and passed down through the generations. They are now being shared as people are building new canoes. It is a time of pride and rich renewal. It is a celebration of life and an example of how the human spirit can survive dramatic change.

# Glossary

**archaeologists**—scientists who study past cultures based on artifacts and other evidence left behind

**artifacts**—objects made or modified by humans

**beluga**—a white whale that lives in the Artic ocean

**dentalia**—horn-shaped shells

**drought**—a lack of rain or water

**excavate**—to scientifically recover and study the remains of past human activity

**keelson**—the long structure fastened to the bottom of a boat to brace the frame

**pautit**—a single double-bladed paddle used by kayakers

**pelts**—animal skins, especially with fur

**prow**—the front end of a boat

**radiocarbon dating**—the method of determining the age of an object by measuring the amount of a radioactive element that is present

**rapids**—the parts of a river where the water surges past sunken rocks or drops over falls

**tules**—large American marsh plants

**umiaks**—open Inuit boats made with wooden frames covered with animal hide

# To Find Out More

## Books

Cooper, Joan. *Canoes and Kayaks*. Vero Beach, Fla.: Rourke, 1999.

Coulter, Tony. *Jacques Cartier, Samuel de Champlain, and the Explorers of Canada*. New York: Chelsea House, 1993.

Doherty, Katherine M., and Craig A. Doherty. *The Wampanoag*. New York: Franklin Watts, 1995.

Fagan, Brian M. *Archaeology: A Brief Introduction*. Reading, Mass.: Addison-Wesley, 1996.

Gleiter, Jan. *Christopher Columbus*. Austin, Tex.: Raintree Steck-Vaughn, 1996.

Harper, Judith E. *Inuits.* Collingwood, Ontario: Smart Apple Media, 1999.

Newman, Shirlee P. *The Inuits.* New York: Franklin Watts, 1993.

Sattler, Helen Roney, and Jean Day Zallinger (illustrator). *The Earliest Americans.* New York: Clarion, 1993.

# Organizations and Online Sites

Canadian Museum of Civilization
100 Laurier Street
P.O. Box 3100
Station B
Hull, Quebec J8X 4H2, Canada
*http://www.cmcc.muse.digital.ca/cmc/cmceng/welcmeng.html*
This museum has done extensive work on native craft, particularly kayaks.

Makah Museum
Bayview Avenue, Highway 112
P.O. Box 160
Neah Bay, WA 98357
*http://www.makah.com/museum.htm*
This center provides information about the Ozette site and the Makah.

Museum of Anthropology
University of British Columbia
6393 N.W. Marine Drive
Vancouver, B.C. V6T 1Z2, Canada
*http://www.moa.ubc.ca/*
This museum has information about ancient sites where well-preserved baskets and fishing lines and tools from thousands of years ago were discovered in mud.

National Museum of the American Indian
The George Gustav Heye Center
Alexander Hamilton U.S. Custom House
One Bowling Green
New York, NY 10004
*http://www.si.edu/nmai/nav.htm*
This museum has an excellent collection of Native American boats.

# A Note on Sources

Like most authors, I have my own way of researching when I write a book. I usually start in the library. Public libraries are great places, because even if they do not have the book you are looking for, they can search other libraries online.

I check scientific journals and popular magazines for related articles. *Archaeology* magazine, published by the Archaeological Institute of America, was particularly useful. This publication is also online at *www.archaeology.org*.

I also talked to other archaeologists who work around the world on shipwrecks and other sites. They offered hints and gave suggestions of people to contact. I learned about the people who still make reed boats in South America from the Internet. Most of the archaeologists I know are always willing to answer questions and help other researchers and students. Remember, archaeologists started me off on my own career when I was ten!

—*James P. Delgado*

# Index

Numbers in *italics* indicate illustrations.

# About the Author

James P. Delgado has worked as a park ranger, a historian, an underwater archaeologist, a teacher, and a museum director. His love of archaeology began when he was ten, and he went on his first dig at age fourteen. Today, he is the executive director of Vancouver Maritime Museum.

James P. Delgado has written eighteen books related to history and underwater archaeology. He is also the author of the Watts Library books *Shipwrecks from the Westward Movement* and *Wrecks of American Warships*. He currently lives in Vancouver, British Columbia.